One day Fox caught
a rabbit.
"Yahoo!" yowled Fox,
"I've got a rabbit."
So he tied him up and
set off for his den.

On the way he met Weasel. "I've got a rabbit," said Fox proudly.

"So I can see," said Weasel, licking his lips. "But what good is a rabbit if you haven't got onions to cook it with?"

"What a good idea," said Fox. "I love rabbit with onions."

So Weasel rushed off and brought back a bag of onions, and off they went into the woods.

There they met Squirrel and Pheasant.

"Fox has caught a rabbit," said Weasel.

"Very nice," they said.

"And Weasel has brought me some onions to cook it with," said Fox.

"I think you should cook it with hazelnuts," said Squirrel.

"And lots of raisins," said Pheasant. "We'll gladly bring you some!"

"Ugh!" said Weasel. "That sounds horrible."

"No, no," said Fox. "I love hazelnuts and raisins."

So off they went — Fox dragging Rabbit, Weasel with his onions, Pheasant with his raisins, and Squirrel with his hazelnuts.

Then they met Turkey. "Fox has caught a rabbit," said Squirrel.

"I can see that," said Turkey.

"And we're all taking him something to cook it with," said Weasel.

"I think you need cranberries," said Turkey, "and I will gladly give you some."

"Thank you kindly, Turkey," said Fox, and off they all went to Fox's den.

"What's going on?" came a squawk from above. It was Crow.

"I've caught a rabbit," said Fox, "and all my kind friends are bringing onions, hazelnuts, raisins, and cranberries to add to the stew."

"What, no spices?" shrieked Crow. "You can't have rabbit stew without spices. I'll bring you some hot sauce."

Fox got out a big pot and filled it with water. He lit a fire under the pot. The animals put the onions and everything else into the pot, and it started to boil. "Any last requests?" chuckled Fox.

"Pepper!" screamed Rabbit. "Lots and lots of pepper!"

"Of course," said Fox. "And now for the most important ingredient of all — YOU!" He lifted up Rabbit to throw him into the pot.

"WAIT!" shouted Crow, Turkey, Squirrel, and Pheasant.

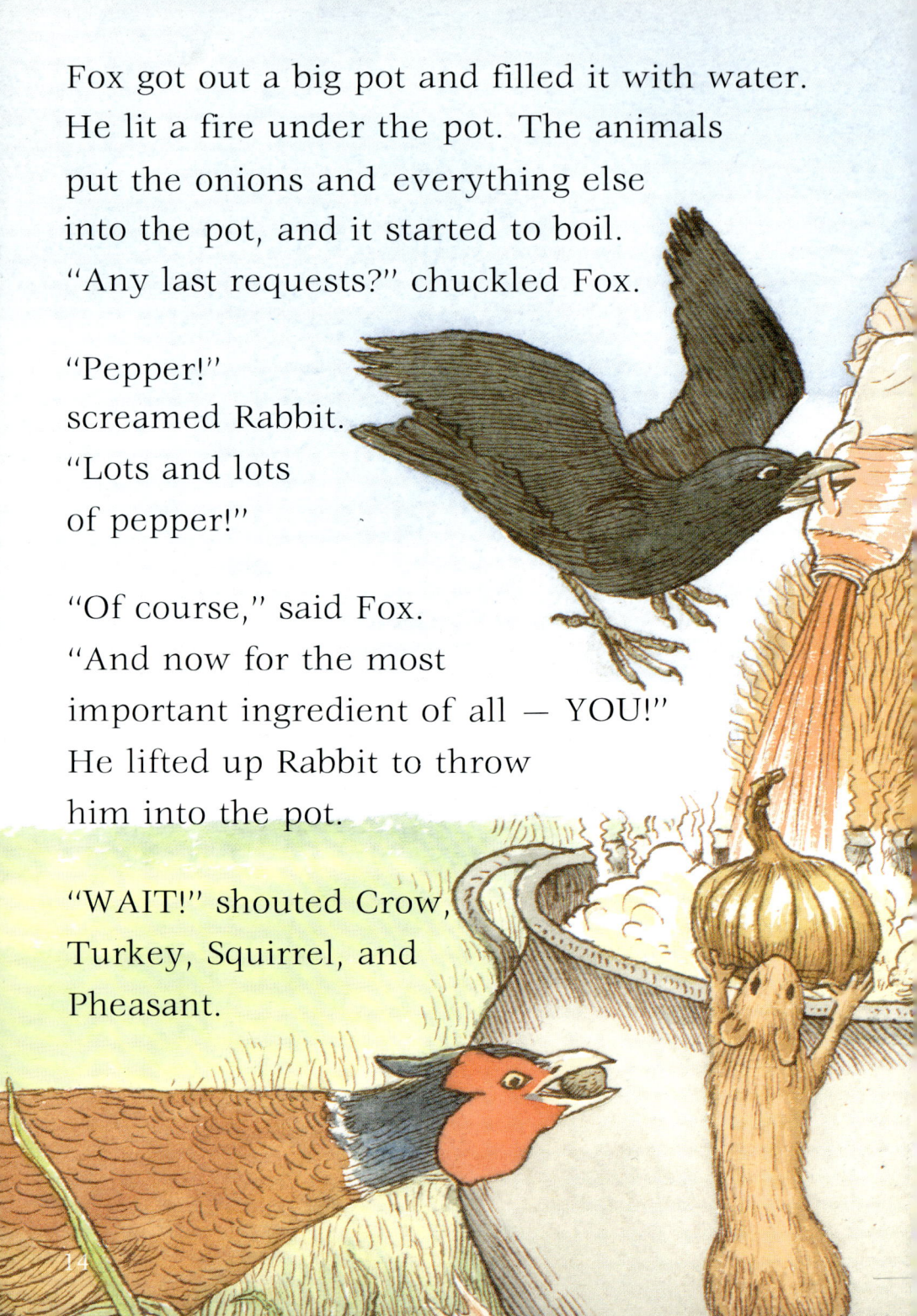

"Aren't you going to taste it before you put him in?" asked Crow.

Crow picked up the spoon, and Fox slurped down a great spoonful of the delicious-looking liquid.

His eyes went red, steam came out of his ears, and he made a sound which started as a growl and ended up as a scream.

"Oh dear! Perhaps he's turning into a dragon," squawked Crow.

"Look at him run!" shouted Squirrel. "He looks like a steam train."

They laughed as they watched Fox run down to the river and jump in.

The friends untied Rabbit and ran, laughing and dancing, around the big pot.
"We got Fox! We got Fox!" they all shouted.

All except Weasel, who slunk off through the undergrowth, with his tummy rumbling.